T0149528

INSPIRED

INSPIRED

THE UMBRELLA OF INSPIRATIONAL PHRASES THAT WILL LAUNCH YOU TO NEW HEIGHTS IN YOUR LIFE

HIAWATHA KENDRICKS-HARRIS

INSPIRED
THE UMBRELLA OF INSPIRATIONAL PHRASES THAT WILL LAUNCH YOU TO NEW HEIGHTS IN YOUR LIFE

iUniverse books may be ordered through booksellers or by contacting:

iUniverse
1663 Liberty Drive
Bloomington, IN 47403
www.iuniverse.com
1-800-Authors (1-800-288-4677)

Because of the dynamic nature of the Internet, any web addresses or links contained in this book may have changed since publication and may no longer be valid. The views expressed in this work are solely those of the author and do not necessarily reflect the views of the publisher, and the publisher hereby disclaims any responsibility for them.

Any people depicted in stock imagery provided by Thinkstock are models, and such images are being used for illustrative purposes only.
Certain stock imagery © Thinkstock.

ISBN: 978-1-5320-3615-6 (sc)
ISBN: 978-1-5320-3616-3 (e)

Print information available on the last page.

iUniverse rev. date: 12/11/2017

Introduction

This book of inspirational phrases is to strengthen, enlighten, encourage and evoke thoughts to help its readers on their journey through life. These phrases will be equally gratifying and motivating.

In this book, you will find powerful & compelling phrases to launch you to new heights in your life.

Acknowledgements

I thank my husband Alphonso "Gift" Harris for his assistance, encouragement and support. I also thank him for his thoughtful and valuable suggestions and comments in preserving and refining my vision for this book.

I thank my mother Chloey Reynolds for her support and guidance. I also thank her for seeing my writing skills at an early age and encouraging me to magnify them in my life.

Dedications

This book is dedicated to my sisters Lovell Kendricks & Deborah Keaton, brother Amsey Keaton, niece Telisha Wynn, as well as, Silk Harris & Vurnette Harris.

The thoughts of our mind wander daily and is not censored, but flows freely. They engage in the activities of our everyday life and hold such deep emotions. To live and not learn from them would be not living at all.

Time is constantly moving. There are no commercials, no pauses, no breaks. Once you enter time, when you are born, there is no turning back only going forward. You cannot recapture time only live in the time remaining. Use time wisely.

Our footsteps are the map to our lives. They show the direction we have been and where we are going. Take each step carefully, for they cannot be repeated or erased.

Feelings, free movement of expressions within that also can be seen outwardly. They capture the inner deepest part of our being; speaking with a voice that is heard through emotions. Feelings, channel them carefully.

Time, precious indeed, linked to what we call life, to live, to be. It is elusive as the air. You cannot see it, touch it, hold it or keep it; you can only be in it. How long is unknown, for everyone has their own. Be mindful of the time you are given and remember each moment is worth living.

Strength, to exist without it is to non-exist within. An attribute that is beneficial to your quality of life and being able to withstand that which is in conflict to you; helping you move through the mixture of emotions, feelings and fears-to stand for your mere existence, strength.

Will is unseen, but strong in nature; its belief is quiet and powerful in existence. Will is to live.

The footprints of our life show the blue prints of our future.

A series of thoughts & images occur in the mind of all; contemplating the possibility of doing something or that something might be. Listening to your inner self will give you the aspiration to achieve a greater part of you.

Life is like a river that flows, it goes in every direction. Its' path is unknown until the destination is reached. We all have a path to travel and must be wise in the direction we choose.

Fear, an invisible imprisonment of oneself that holds your mind hostage; hindering awareness, perception and the faculty of consciousness. Channel your fear to something constructive; never let fear control you.

The hands of time cannot recapture that which was and no longer exist. It cannot move backward, but only forward. The hands of time are for us to be, but not indefinitely.

Words come in many shades of emotions that are felt by the heart flow. The rhythm of such is set by the feelings inside. The spoken cannot be returned, for once said, it is done. Choose your words carefully.

The past is behind us, the present is upon us and the future does not exist until we get there. Be aware of the things you learned in your past, you have in your present and you are bringing to your future.

Everyone has a gift waiting to be unwrapped and shared with others. A natural ability or talent to do something that is uniquely theirs. Unwrap the gift that is inside of you.

Time is the hour glass full of sand, constantly moving, showing that the existence of time is forever fleeting, use it wisely.

Decisions, difficult they can sometimes be, but must be made indeed. Inner thoughts of choices to make, and contemplating which one to take. In the conclusion of what to do, let your intuitions see you through.

The beginning of life is entering a story that is created by its author, you. This story is written and rewrote to search for its true purpose. Know the contents of yourself and define that which you believe is your purpose.

Be inspired daily, for inspiration brings forth a higher level of creativity with the belief that you can accomplish anything.

When deciding which road to travel, remember you are the driving force of your ambitions to your destiny.

The school of life is attended every day by each of us. We need no books, papers or pencils, only ourselves. It's never closed, for it is open 24 hours. It has many teachers and many lessons to learn. There are no grades to give, for how can you score how you live. The school of life we all must attend, starting with the day we are born until the end.

Attitude, your approach to your belief is seen through your attitude. Your demeanor can speak a volume of words. The view-point you have is shown through your reaction, be mindful of the way you present yourself.

In life, there is only a one-way ticket, no round trip. Give it your best shot.

Become who you are meant to be through conscious reflection, self-alignment, and have self-directed changes in your path that will allow you to grow.

Sight, are we that have visual perception blinded and those without sight are not? For having sight does not mean we have vision which allows us to pursue our dreams and achieve our goals, know the difference. The capacity to gain an accurate and deep intuitive understanding of oneself requires insight. Have vision to see all you can be and move forward with excellency.

Each moment you live, live it victoriously; for the present is all you have and the future is only a wish with the hope of longevity.

Make the decision to allow yourself the thought of reaching your goals, for a mental block will stop progress; be absolute in obtaining them.

Life, what is it to you? Growth, changes or just your existence? A time to explore who you are or the time between the dash when you are born and live no more? Whatever, it may be to each person, it is always a gift to live. LIFE – Live It Fully Everyday...

Motivation is the engine that propels us forward into our visions. It gives us the enthusiasm, drive, initiative and willingness to accomplish our dreams, be motivated.

The true essence of a person is that quality that is indispensable; the quality that is their signature in life.

If it is not in your vision, make no decision. To receive desired results, you must know your objective.

Live life with a sense of urgency for it passes quickly. Living with urgency will compel you to take immediate action on things you otherwise would not.

We live in time; a continued progression of existence that we create the events for our life. Time is precious and fleeting; by its very nature passes and cannot return. Plan your time carefully.

Contemplate where you are and have a vision where you want to be. Project the qualities you embody and give life to them; as well, they will give life to you.

Set yourself free from things that will not allow you to be your best, for these things will deprive you of confidence, hope and spirit of bringing forth excellence in yourself.

Each day brings a new adventure to learn from or conquer. Follow your heart and be optimistic.

Do not limit yourself by lack of knowledge, but expand your mind and challenge yourself to learn more.

Recognize who you are and in doing so you will realize the person you can become.

Define your passion and you will find that which defines you.

Life is a race, do not be a spectator watching your life unfold; claim your position and blaze your own trails.

Opinions, through the eyes of others. Is it for us to be what they see, or to choose our own destiny? Be in control of self.

Changes, although apprehensive in making them, we all must consider them for the advancement and development of our lives. Welcome change, allow growth.

Have the drive to move ahead, the vision to follow your dreams and the ambition to obtain that which you seek.

During life trials and tribulations, be wise. Go forward with zest and zeal, with a sense of who you are and a purpose.

Do not always put your breaks on; get your mileage out of life and live.

Memories, notes from time past, invisible, but seen in the minds of all. Learn from that which is concealed from sight, but visible in thought, for they are our memories.

Celebrate what makes you different and access what makes you unique.

Excuses are the enemy of execution for they will stop you from getting things done.

You are dealt many hands in life and sometimes they can be stacked against you; given the right attitude you can have a hand well played.

Do not be burdened with things of the past; live in the present and plan the future.

It is not the years in your life that count, it is the life you put in the years you live.

Make a commitment to that which you desire to do and be not wasteful of time which is precious to you.

Know the object of your ambition, for it is that knowledge which will define your purpose

Life's detours can slow down that which need to be done, but not stop that which you are determined to do; be persistent and claim you victory.

Stay strong in your convictions, wise in your decisions and confident in your belief.

Life begins with a question mark and ends with a period, in between is for time to live. Live the life you want to be your legacy.

Refresh yourself with joy, hold on to that which makes you wiser and be optimistic.

Life's canvas is open to ideas and opportunities. You are the artist; design the life you envision.

Accept the positive and reject the negative. Positive thinking improves one's state of mind; negative thinking diminishes it.

An investment in you will yield earnings and cause growth.

Life, like a vapor in the wind it comes and goes quickly. Live it with heart and soul.

There is no refund on time so spend it carefully.

Do not minimize what you do, but maximize all you do. Give it 100 percent.

Life is not to pass by and reclaim. There is no reimbursement and it cannot be compensated with anything else, cherish it.

Make sacrifices for your visions and dreams and be empowered through them to make that which seems impossible, possible.

Achievement and success are in the power of those who dare to dream and then making their dream a reality.

Rise high when you are feeling low; stand tall when you are feeling small, for you are resilient, phenomenal you are.

Do not limit your vision, see more than you know is possible and do more than you think you can.

Develop a method to obtain your objective; adhere to a plan that will let your vision stand.

Do not let others dim the light inside of you; always let your light shine.

Living life is like exercising, you must have endurance.

Take inventory of your life so you can see the things you have done and still need to do. Recognize all your glory, so you can recognize the gift inside of you.

Do not be discouraged by disappointments or rejections for they are both factors to build character and strength.

Circumstances are the conditions of what is, but not what will be, believe in you.

Do not always be the man in the mirror, but also be the man holding the mirror so others can see the reflection of themselves.

Only a shell you see, not what is inside of me or who I can be, do you even know my destiny? Do not let the views of others dictate your life.

We all have a personal journey and must stake claim to it; for being passive, our life will be chosen for us by default.

Do not be tempted to live without a purpose, for it is with purpose that we excel into a greater sense of who we are.

Life is to live; it embraces the soul and brings that which is within to consciousness. Awareness of life is awareness of you, for you exist through your life and your life exists through you, treasure it.

Who are you? Do you believe in what you see and able to choose your own destiny or even know what is within you to be? Who are you? Be in touch with yourself.

Do things that open your mind and let your expressions come through.

Moments of reflection are needed to see in the mirror clearly.

Life is given to us. It does not come with a bow or neatly wrapped or filled with all the things we think life should be. It is a gift, cherish it.

Be optimistic of the possibilities and move forward.

Challenges are like exams; we are tested to establish our true capabilities.

Profit from the changes in your life when action is taken, for life is change and change is life and with that is growth.

The psyche is the puppet master that pulls the strings to our being. It is the mind, ego, and subconscious. It is you, know who you are.

Your self-talk will be the evidence of your life achievements.

Within each moment you live there is an opportunity; it can be a path to success or a road to failure. The direction you travel is your choice.

Live now or forever hold your peace; you have one shot make it count.

Thinking is good, but resting in thought is not; you might sleep on your dreams and never have a vision, do not procrastinate.

Adversity is opposed to one's best interest; stand strong in the face of it.

Move yourself forward, be positive, live fully, be willing and most of all be inspired.

We awake each day not knowing what it will bring, but moving ahead and sorting through it as we go. Be aware of what is presented in your day and ask not for the reason, but rather the knowledge and understanding to handle each situation.

Along the highway of life there are many signs; detour ahead, stop, no right turn, do not enter, dead end, wrong way and keep right, among many others. Adhere to these signs and be aware of their true meaning for the road we travel is defined by the choices we make.

Life can be perplexing, bewildering and baffling. It requires ingenuity and persistence to form the life we desire. Success may not occur at first, but with effort, patience and faith it will.

Happiness is the pleasure you feel inside that captures your well-being and gives you enjoyment in the things you do. It enhances the quality of your life, for you are rejoicing within. Be free to be happy.

The pages of life turn every day and with each turn there is another time to write in the pages of life. As the pages accumulate, numbers reflect the time that has gone by. Your life can be shown as you want it to be or by just existing. Be thoughtful in your pages of life.

Do not push the delete bottom on your dreams,
because of someone else's vision for you.

See yourself in the light you want to reflect.

Achievement and success are in the power of those who dare to dream.

Dedicate yourself to be the very best; reach for the stars and the light will shine on you.

Greatness is in those who believe in themselves and know of the greatness that is within them to achieve.

Daily choices influence your life's outcome.

*Be liberated from your own fears and
hopeful in everything you do.*

If you are lost in your troubles, be found in your joy.

Believe in yourself and act upon that belief.

A firmness of purpose will lead to many achievements.

I was a caterpillar, but now I am a butterfly
spreading my wings with beautiful colors
for all to see-know the beauty in you.

Conclusion

When we are inspired, that phenomenal quality that arises in us where our creativeness is aroused, we begin to explore the depth of our ability to achieve our goals. Inspirations serve to encourage, energize, exhilarate and motivate us into our dreams, bringing our visions into existence. Always be inspired for it is the key to unlock the door to who you are and can be.